A CourseGuide for

God's Word Alone

Matthew Barrett

ZONDERVAN
ACADEMIC

ZONDERVAN ACADEMIC

A CourseGuide for God's Word Alone

Copyright © 2020 by Zondervan

Requests for information should be addressed to:
Zondervan, *3900 Sparks Dr. SE, Grand Rapids, Michigan 49546*

ISBN 978-0-310-11060-6 (softcover)

Printed in the United States of America

CONTENTS

Introduction

Welcome to *A CourseGuide for God's Word Alone*. These guides were created for formal and informal students alike who want to engage deeper in biblical, theological, or ministry studies. We hope this guide will provide an opportunity for you to grow not only in your understanding, but also in your faith.

How to Use This Guide

This guide is meant to be used in conjunction with the book *God's Word Alone* and its corresponding videos, *God's Word Alone Video Lectures*. After you have read each chapter in the book and watched the accompanying video lesson, the materials in this guide will help you review and assess what you have learned. Application-oriented questions are included as well.

Each CourseGuide has been individually designed to best equip you in your studies, but in general, you can expect the following components. Most CourseGuides begin every chapter with a "You Should Know" section, which highlights key terminology, people, and facts to remember. This section serves as a helpful summary for directing your studies. Reflection questions, typically two to three per chapter, prompt you to summarize key points you've learned. Discussion questions invite you to an even deeper level of engagement. Finally, most chapters will end with a short quiz to test your retention. You can find the answer key to each quiz at the bottom of the page following it.

For Further Study

CourseGuides accompany books and videos from some of the world's top biblical and theological scholars. They may be used independently, or in small groups or classrooms, offering quality instruction to equip students for academic and ministry pursuits. If you would like to engage in further study with Zondervan's CourseGuides, the full lineup may be viewed online. After completing your studies with *A CourseGuide for God's Word Alone*, we recommend moving on to *A CourseGuide for Faith Alone*, and *A CourseGuide for Christ Alone*.

Introduction to
God's Word Alone

You Should Know

- The implications of *sola Scriptura*: Scripture alone is our final authority; Scripture alone is our sufficient authority; Scripture alone is our inerrant authority

- *Sola Scriptura* acknowledges that there are other important authorities for the Christian that should be listened to and followed.

- The Roman Church of Martin Luther's day affirmed with him Scripture's divine authority and inspiration. What made Luther's stance on biblical authority so different and so offensive to the Roman Church was his insistence that Scripture alone is the inerrant authority.

- *Sola Scriptura*: *only Scripture*, because it is God's inspired Word and our inerrant, sufficient, and final authority

- Inerrancy: the necessary corollary of inspiration Scenario

Essay Questions

Short

1. What are the three implications Barrett extracts from the meaning of *sola Scriptura*? Does *sola Scriptura* acknowledge the existence and legitimacy of other authorities for the Christian? Explain your answer.

2. Are inspiration and inerrancy linked? How does this question relate to the Bible's authority?

3. Summarize the thoughts of the Chicago Statement on Inerrancy and the Cambridge Declaration on the relationship between Scripture's authority and inerrancy. Do you agree with their conclusions? Why or why not?

Long

1. Referencing Scripture, make a case for or against Scripture's self-authenticating nature (i.e., internally derived authority). Should we believe the Bible because it says so or because some other entity, individual or corporate, says so?

Quiz

1. (T/F) The sixteenth-century Roman Catholic Church believed Scripture itself was inspired by God and therefore inerrant.

2. (T/F) *Nuda Scriptura* means that the Bible is our chief, supreme, and ultimate authority.

3. (T/F) While church tradition and church officials play a *magisterial* role, Scripture alone plays a *ministerial* role.

4. (T/F) Luther's stance on Scripture was so detested by Rome because he believed *only* Scripture is the *inerrant* authority.

5. (T/F) God's Word is inherently and invariably *Unitarian* in nature.

6. (T/F) In the wake of Rome's muddy Tiber and postmodernism's murky waters, few doctrines have been so quickly dismantled as the *clarity* of Scripture.

7. The abandonment of biblical authority began with _____.

    a) The Enlightenment
    b) The Reformation
    c) Theological Liberalism
    d) Postmodernism

8. _____ means that *only Scripture*, because it is God's inspired Word, is our inerrant, sufficient, and final authority for the church.

   a) *Sola gratia*
   b) *Sola Scriptura*
   c) *Sola fide*
   d) *Sola Christus*

9. Which is *not* one of the implications of *sola Scriptura*?

   a) Scripture alone plays a ministerial role.
   b) Scripture alone is our final authority.
   c) Scripture alone is our sufficient authority.
   d) Scripture alone is our inerrant authority.

10. What church document states the following: "The *authority* of Scripture is inescapably impaired if this total divine *inerrancy* is in any way limited or disregarded"?

   a) The Belgic Confession
   b) The Westminster Confession of Faith
   c) The Chicago Statement on Inerrancy
   d) The Book of Concord

CHAPTER 1

The Road to Reformation

Biblical Authority in the Sixteenth Century

You Should Know

- The issues discussed in Luther's Ninety-Five Theses: the abuse of indulgences; supposed papal authority over purgatory; whether the pope truly had the sinner's welfare in mind

- The events of the Reformation in chronological sequence: the Great Western Schism; Luther posting his Ninety-Five Theses on the Castle Church door in Wittenberg; the Leipzig debate; the Diet of Worms; the First Zurich Disputation; Rome's declaration of papal infallibility as official dogma

- The events of the Reformation Bible in chronological sequence: John Wycliffe publishes the first English Bible; Desiderius Erasmus' Greek New Testament is published; Luther publishes his German translation of the New Testament; William Tyndale publishes his English translation of the New Testament; William Tyndale publishes his English translation of the Pentateuch; Luther publishes his German translation of the Bible

- Contrary to Rome, Luther argued that God's Word alone is the church's inerrant authority.

- Luther was condemned as a heretic by Rome in Leipzig.

- Tradition 1: Tradition is subject to Scripture because only Scripture is the inerrant and infallible written source of God's revelation to his people.

- Tradition 2: Divine revelation has two sources: Scripture and ecclesiastical Tradition, including the pope and the magisterium.

- Those who chose the pope as the church's final authority were called curialists, while those who chose church councils were called conciliarists.

- Characteristic of the Spiritualist Thomas Müntzer's beliefs: Elevated new revelations from the Spirit over the old written text; stated that Scripture is nothing more than ink on paper; believed that God's people needed a new "Daniel"; shared the view with Rome that Scripture was not enough and needed an inspired interpreter

Essay Questions

Short

1. Explain why Luther believed that *sola Scriptura* was directly connected to the inerrancy of Scripture. On the topic of inerrancy, what did Luther believe concerning church councils and popes?

2. Explain both Tradition 1 and Tradition 2. Which one did Luther and the Reformers affirm? What kind of "authority" does the church have in Tradition 1?

3. Describe each of the three types of radical reformers.

Long

1. Were the Reformers inventing something new in the doctrine of *sola Scriptura*? What were they trying to do? The last council of Rome, Vatican II (1962–65), continued Rome's rejection of *sola Scriptura*. Referencing what Scripture says of itself, answer the question, "Is *sola Scriptura* necessary for the Christian faith?"

Quiz

1. (T/F) The view that tradition is subject to Scripture because only Scripture is the inerrant and infallible written source of God's revelation to his people is called Tradition 2.

2. (T/F) At the First Zurich Disputation, Zwingli was careful to avoid *nuda Scriptura*.

3. (T/F) The Reformation slogan "Scripture interprets Scripture" conveys only the idea that correct biblical interpretation requires that we submit ourselves to the Bible's interpretation of us.

4. Which was *not* one of the three radical reformer groups mentioned in this unit?
   a) The Anabaptists
   b) The Spiritualists
   c) The Evangelical Rationalists
   d) The Lollards

5. Who published the first English New Testament and Pentateuch translated directly from the Greek and Hebrew respectively?
   a) John Wycliffe
   b) William Tyndale
   c) Martin Luther
   d) Desiderius Erasmus

6. Who accused Cardinal Jacopo Sadoleto of misconstruing the proper relationship and order between the Spirit, the Word, and the church?
   a) John Calvin
   b) Martin Luther
   c) William Tyndale
   d) Huldrych Zwingli

7. Which is *not* one of the points extracted from Calvin's *Institutes* regarding *sola Scriptura*?
   a) Scripture is the Word of God.
   b) Scripture receives its authority not from the church but from God.

c) Scripture's credibility depends on man's reason and the Spirit's testimony.

d) Scripture is our infallible and inerrant authority.

8. Which is one of the scriptural passages pivotal to Roman doctrine that Luther addressed in the Leipzig debate?

a) John 20:13–16

b) Matthew 16:18–19

c) Matthew 28:16–20

d) John 20:23

9. In which of the three treatises leading up to the Diet of Worms did Luther assert that good works do not merit righteousness but are the fruit that comes from being declared righteous?

a) *The Freedom of a Christian*

b) *The Babylonian Captivity of the Church*

c) *Exsurge, Domine*

d) *To the Christian Nobility of the German Nation*

10. Who did Huldrych Zwingli say influenced his turn to Reformation theology?

a) Martin Luther

b) Jan Hus

c) John Calvin

d) Desiderius Erasmus

CHAPTER 2

The Modern Shift in Authority

The Enlightenment, Liberalism, and Liberalism's Nemeses

You Should Know

- Characteristics of Karl Barth's neo-orthodoxy: a "theology from above" should be restored; the *Logos* takes on three forms; Scripture is errant; Christ is the Word of God.

- For Barth, the Bible may become the Word of God as God himself uses it in the world.

- Many contemporary evangelicals find Barth's doctrine of Scripture problematic because he seems to rely upon inerrancy even though he denies it doctrinally, his view of Scripture is driven by a mistaken view of God's free will, and his view of Scripture fails to match Jesus's own view of Scripture.

- The five points of The Five Point Declaration: the inspiration and inerrancy of Scripture; the virgin birth of Christ; the substitutionary atonement of Christ; the bodily (historical) resurrection of Christ; the miracles of Christ

- Characteristics of Machen's response to liberalism: Protestant liberalism is another religion altogether; liberalism was driven by naturalistic presuppositions; the "religious experience" of liberalism was not Christian; plenary inspiration and inerrancy go hand-in-hand.

- Rationalist biblical criticism: an approach that elevated reason above Scripture as its judge and critic

- Protestant liberalism: An intentional renovation of Christian orthodoxy to accommodate Enlightenment thought

- Deism: the belief that God created the world to run on its own, apart from his supernatural intervention or providential involvement. Deists were critical of special revelation since it involved God's supernatural intervention into history. They also argued that human reason is our judge, even over Scripture.

Essay Questions

Short

1. How did the Enlightenment view reason? What does this view mean for the Bible's necessity and sufficiency?

2. Contrast a "theology from below" with a "theology from above" (91–92).

3. How did the spirit of Schleiermacher's liberalism live on in Ritschl, Harnack, and Herrmann? (99–100)

Long

1. Outline "Old Princeton's Bulwark," including the modernist objections to the views of its constituents. Also, summarize J. Gresham Machen's criticism of liberalism.

Quiz

1. (T/F) "New papalism" refers to the supposed infallibility of the biblical scholar.

2. (T/F) Theism differs from deism because theism is the belief that God created the world to run on its own, apart from his supernatural intervention or providential involvement.

3. (T/F) Protestant liberalism advocated a "theology from above."

4. The _____ individual believed he could have access to pure human reason, which would allow him to tear down traditional ecclesiastical myths that only served to oppress societies of ages past.

    a) Renaissance
    b) Postmodern
    c) Enlightenment
    d) Reformation

5. Which is *not* one of the stages in the Enlightenment's reappraisal and criticism of traditional Christianity identified by Alister McGrath?

    a) The "beliefs of Christianity" are "rational."
    b) Christian fundamentals can be "derived from reason itself."
    c) Reason is above divine revelation, sitting as its judge.
    d) Spiritual revelation is necessary to comprehend universal truths.

6. Who planted the seed that eventually produced rational biblical criticism (RBC)?

    a) Baruch Spinoza
    b) Martin Luther
    c) Desiderius Erasmus
    d) Johannes von Eck

7. The Enlightenment's complete reliance on reason made it skeptical towards _____.

    a) History
    b) Absolute truth
    c) Empiricism
    d) Rational biblical criticism

8. Who took special revelation off the throne of authority and replaced it with man's experience?

    a) G. E. Lessing
    b) Friedrich Schleiermacher

   c) F. C. Baur
   d) David F. Strauss

9. Who, borrowing heavily from Hegel's dialectical philosophy, concluded that the New Testament tells us very little about the historical Jesus because Peter and Paul were competing sources?

   a) David F. Strauss
   b) Albert Schweitzer
   c) F. C. Bauer
   d) Julius Wellhausen

10. What event ended Karl Barth's infatuation with liberalism?

   a) World War I
   b) World War II
   c) The Boer War
   d) The Defenestration of Prague

CHAPTER 3

Today's Crisis over Biblical Authority

Evangelicalism's Apologetic and the Postmodern Turn

You Should Know

- Postconservatives do not treat the Bible as first-order language that is fully authoritative. Postconservatives embrace a constructionist view.

- Hermeneutical nonrealism: the truth of an interpretation depends on the response of the reader.

- Postmoderns view all explanations of reality as constructions that are useful but not objectively true. Postmoderns deny that we have the ability to step outside our constructions of reality.

- Postmodernism's core tenets: all explanations of reality are useful constructions; there is no objective truth; meaning emerges only as the interpreter enters into dialogue with the text (poststructuralism or deconstructionism); no one can step outside their view of reality

- Modernism assumed man could obtain cognitive certainty due to the objective nature of knowledge itself.

- Core tenets of the Age of Reason (a.k.a., the Enlightenment, modernism): reason stands apart from faith and revelation; man can acquire objective truth; the world, by nature, possesses structure and order, apart from humanity's involvement; reason is completely neutral and omnicompetent

9. Which two statements are key presuppositions of postmodernism? (pg. 134)

   a) Postmoderns view all explanations of reality as constructions that are useful but not objectively true.
   b) Postmoderns deny that we have the ability to step outside our constructions of reality.
   c) Postmoderns view all explanations of reality as constructions that are objectively true in and of themselves.
   d) Postmoderns affirm that we have the ability to step outside our constructions of reality.

10. According to _____ Grenz and Franke, Scripture is inspired and authoritative only in the sense that the Spirit speaks to the community through the Bible, not because the Bible is inherently God-breathed (pg. 137–138).

   a) Foundationalists
   b) Postconservatives
   c) New Evangelicals
   d) hermeneutical nonrealists

CHAPTER 4

God's Word in the Economy of the Gospel

Covenant, Trinity, and the Necessity of a Saving Word

You Should Know

- The all-too-common temptation is to think that divine revelation is God's response to us. However, we do not find God. God finds us and makes himself known to us. God has made himself known to us in a saving way.

- General revelation is God's revelation of his divine attributes. It is given to all humanity and is revealed both in nature and in humanity's conscience.

- The attributes of God that he reveals through general revelation: Sustainer, Immanent, Good, Righteous, Sovereign

- Humanity's sense of the divine: knowledge of a Creator ingrained and embedded into humanity's moral nature

- Man's sense of the divine becomes all the more apparent when he sins.

- Romans 1:21–32 explains that even though man has a knowledge of God, he suppresses that knowledge and instead lives for himself.

- Creator-creature distinction: God is infinite and we are finite. Our knowledge of God is completely dependent upon God giving it to us.

- Special revelation is necessary, because the Creator-creature distinction requires God to take the initiative; humanity's sinfulness necessitates God's revelation of himself in a saving way; general revelation is insufficient for salvation; and special revelation is redemptive in nature.

- Scripture is Christocentric and Christotelic.

- The form and progression of special revelation in redemptive history: covenants are the context for God's revelation of himself; Jesus Christ is the climax of God's revelation; God's permanent revelation of himself is Scripture; Jesus Christ is the theme of God's revelation

Essay Questions

Short

1. Provide a rundown of God's divine attributes. Many of these attributes come from Paul's speech at the Areopagus (Acts 17:22–31). Why do you think Paul may have discussed God's divine attributes in this context?

2. Identify and explain the two reasons why God must find us and reveal himself to us, and not the other way around.

3. Describe the Trinitarian nature of revelation.

Long

1. What does general revelation tell us about God, and how and to whom it is revealed? Why do you think general revelation is necessary, and is general revelation sufficient to save us? How does special revelation factor into this discussion?

Quiz

1. (T/F) It is enough to say the biblical authors wrote about God or even wrote for God.

2. (T/F) Knowledge of a Creator is ingrained and embedded into humanity's moral nature.

3. What can we say about general revelation?

   a) General revelation is God's revelation of his divine and human attributes.
   b) General revelation is given to all and is revealed both in nature and in humanity's conscience.
   c) General revelation communicates the gospel of Jesus Christ.
   d) General revelation alone is sufficient for God's purposes in redemptive history.

4. Which is *not* true of God according to general revelation and Scripture?

   a) He is created.
   b) He is immanent.
   c) He is righteous.
   d) He is sovereign.

5. What are the reason(s) why God must find us and reveal himself to us?

   a) The Creator-creature distinction
   b) Humanity's sinfulness
   c) The sufficiency of general revelation to save us
   d) Both A & B
   e) Both A & C

6. Which is *not* one of the ways God has communicated through history?

   a) Automatic writing
   b) Theophanies
   c) Miracles and mighty acts/events
   d) Scripture

7. God's communication of himself (Word) comes to us in the context of _____.

   a) Covenants
   b) Dispensations

c) Epochs
d) Eons

8. Which statement does *not* speak to the inseparable connection between Word and covenant?

a) God declares what he will do through covenant promises.
b) God accomplishes what he said he would do.
c) God leaves it up to mankind to figure out what his mighty acts mean.
d) God communicates what his mighty acts mean and how to apply them.

9. God's special revelation of himself is by nature _____.

a) Arian
b) Monophysitic
c) Trinitarian
d) Modalistic

10. Which person of the Trinity assumes the central role in delivering divine revelation in regard to Scripture?

a) The Father
b) The Holy Spirit
c) The Son
d) All of the above

CHAPTER 5

God Speaks Covenantal Words

Creation, Fall, and the Longing of a Better World

You Should Know

- Aspects of the Lord's covenant with Adam: given dominion over the created order; placed in the garden; instructed to work and keep the garden; and prohibited from eating from the tree of the knowledge of good and evil

- *Protoevangelium*: "the first gospel" found in Genesis 3:15

- The narrowed lineage of the promised seed of the *protoevangelium*: Abraham, the tribe of Judah, and Jesus Christ

- Aspects of the Lord's covenant with Noah: preservation of the woman's seed; creation renewal; promise to never flood the earth again; recapitulation of the dominion mandate (multiply, fill the earth, and subdue it)

- Abrahamic covenant: The Lord promises Abraham land, seed, and universal blessing.

- The ratification ceremony of the Abrahamic covenant teaches that God is a true and faithful God who initiates his promises and fulfills them in every detail.

- The first covenant where God's revelation is *explicitly* one of special saving grace, of God calling a specific people to himself, to be his own chosen people, is the Abrahamic covenant.

- God warned Joshua to be careful to do all that was in the law of Moses, not letting the Book of the Law depart from his mouth. Joshua was to meditate on it day and night (Josh. 1:7–8). He engraved on stones a copy of the law, and he read all the words of the law before all the assembly of Israel. Joshua viewed the Book of the Law as the Word of God.

- Expanding on the Abrahamic covenant, the Davidic covenant includes the promise that the Lord will establish the kingdom of his offspring forever.

Essay Questions

Short

1. Explain why God made a covenant with Adam in the garden. Contrast and compare the language of the Noahic covenant with the Adamic covenant. What key word is found in the Noahic covenant but not in the Adamic covenant?

2. In the Ten Commandments, what did the people of God have for the first time? What is "astonishing" about this account?

3. How did the prophets communicate that their words were indeed God's Word? How did this separate them from the false prophets?

Long

1. Provide the context of the *protoevangelion*. Then trace the lineage of the "seed of the woman" throughout redemptive history with Scripture references.

Quiz

1. (T/F) God brought Adam into a specific and special covenant from the start.

2. (T/F) What is remarkable about the Lord cutting a covenant with Abraham is that it is the Lord who passes between the hewn animal carcasses instead of Abraham.

3. (T/F) The covenant Word written on tablets (i.e., the Ten Commandments) is *holy* and *temporary*.

4. What is Genesis 3:15 ("And I will put enmity between you and the woman, and between your offspring and hers; he will crush your head, and you will strike his heel") known as?

   a) *Communicatum idiomatum*
   b) *Vocatio*
   c) *Sensus divinitatis*
   d) *Protoevangelium*

5. Following humanity's dispersion at Babel, what person did the Lord choose through whom all of the earth would be blessed rather than cursed?

   a) Noah
   b) Abraham
   c) Seth
   d) Moses

6. What separates the Lord's covenant with Abraham from his covenant with Noah?

   a) A special saving relationship
   b) The word *everlasting*
   c) A gracious character
   d) A new creation

7. Which does *not* happen during the Exodus?

   a) God brings plagues on Egypt
   b) God divides the Red Sea
   c) God hardens Moses's heart
   d) God guides the Israelites with pillars of cloud and fire

8. In the Ten Commandments, the people had for the first time:

   a) The Word of God in written form
   b) The Word of God communicated to them directly

c) The Word of God
d) Instruction from God

9. Where is God's commandment according to Deuteronomy 30:11–14?

a) In heaven
b) Beyond the sea
c) In those who are circumcised in the flesh
d) In the mouths and hearts of those circumcised in the heart

10. According to Barrett, David's reign as a whole is characterized by his attention to _____.

a) The Word of God
b) The word of Moses
c) The people of Israel
d) Defeating Israel's enemies

CHAPTER 6

God's Covenantal Word Proves True

Christ, the Word Made Flesh

You Should Know

- Sequence: List the covenantal events in chronological order: God covenants with Adam; God covenants with Abraham; God gives Moses the Ten Commandments; God covenants with David; God cuts the new covenant by sacrificing his only begotten Son

- The covenant cut by Christ is the new covenant that all the previous covenants anticipate and typify.

- The language of John 1:1 echoes Genesis 1.

- Christ's threefold office includes the roles of prophet, priest, and king.

- In the incarnation we receive the most incredible revelation of all.

- The three points given by Barrett that help us understand the advent of Christ leading up to the written Word of the New Testament Scriptures: (1) Christ fulfilled the Old Testament promises of God, (2) Christ is the full revelation of God, and (3) the Father and the Son sent the Spirit of truth with a word of truth.

- The Word: Jesus Christ who fulfilled the Old Testament promises of God and affirmed them as the very Word of God

- Scripture makes no stronger statement about the ongoing authority of the Torah than Matthew 5:18: "For truly I tell you, until heaven and earth disappear, not the smallest letter, not the least stroke of a pen, will by any means disappear from the Law until everything is accomplished."

- Some ways that Jesus fulfilled the Old Testament promises of God: he announced that Isaiah 61:1 was fulfilled in the assembly's hearing; he declared that he did not come to abolish the Law but to fulfill it; he predicts his death and resurrection; he told Nicodemus that, like the bronze serpent, he too must be lifted up

- Divine revelation's Trinitarian nature: The Father planned, the Son brought to completion, and the Spirit reminds God's people of Jesus's teachings.

Essay Questions

Short

1. Why did John apply the title "Word" to Jesus?

2. In what way did John 3 show that not only oracles but Old Testament events and symbols prefigured Christ?

3. How does Barrett respond to some neo-orthodox theologians' claims that Jesus is the Word but Scripture itself is not?

Long

1. Detail the Old Testament covenants from Adam to David (including the giving of the Law, a.k.a. the Sinaitic or Mosaic covenant). Explain how the New Testament reveals Jesus Christ as the fulfillment of God's covenant promises.

Quiz

1. (T/F) The significance of Moses and Elijah during the Transfiguration is that they represent the Law and the Prophets respectively, meaning that Jesus is the culmination of both.

2. (T/F) The apostolic testimony to the gospel and the resurrection of Christ is entirely dependent upon the inspiration of the Old Testament.

3. (T/F) Jesus only came as a priest and king, but not as a prophet.

4. Which Gospel especially shows that Jesus is the long-awaited Messiah?

   a) Matthew
   b) Mark
   c) John
   d) Luke

5. It is because the Word is _____ that he can make the Father known in a way that has never been done before.

   a) The Son
   b) Man
   c) The Christ
   d) God

6. Which is *not* one of the points discussed by Barrett about the advent of Christ leading up to the New Testament's written Word?

   a) The Father draws his people unto himself by enabling them to come to Jesus Christ, the Word.
   b) Christ, the Word, fulfilled the promises of God in the Old Testament, which he affirmed as the very Word of God.
   c) Christ, as the Son of God and the Word of God, is the ultimate, climactic, and full revelation of God, and his word is true because it came from the Father.
   d) The Father and Son sent the Spirit of truth with a word of truth.

7. It is in the Word made flesh that the Word of God prior to Christ finds its _____.

   a) *Homoousios*
   b) *Homoiousios*
   c) *Telos*
   d) *Eschatoevangelium*

8. What event, alluded to in John 3, serves as a reminder that not only prophetic predictions but also events and symbols in the Old Testament prefigured Christ?

    a) Moses striking the rock at Meribah
    b) The bronze serpent
    c) Abraham sacrificing Isaac on Mt. Moriah
    d) The Day of Atonement

9. The Son came to make the _____ known.

    a) Spirit
    b) Word
    c) Father
    d) Son

10. Where did Jesus tell the disciples that unless he went away, the Holy Spirit would not come?

    a) John 16:7
    b) John 16:12–15
    c) John 14:26
    d) John 15:26

CHAPTER 7

God Speaks with Authority

The Inspiration of Scripture

You Should Know

- 2 Timothy 3:16: "All Scripture is God-breathed and is useful for teaching, rebuking, correcting and training in righteousness."

- According to Barrett, verbal plenary inspiration theory is the correct theory of inspiration.

- It is the very words themselves that are breathed out by God, and this means that we should never pit plenary inspiration against verbal inspiration.

- Some may be tempted to think that the human authors wrote their books, and God saw what they wrote after the fact and decided he would adopt it.

- Dual authorship of Scripture: each biblical book has both a divine author and a human author

- Concursive involvement means that Scripture is the product of divine activities working confluently with the human authors.

- *Organic* was the term Kuyper and Bavinck used to describe the relationship between God and the human authors of the Bible.

- Divine accommodation incorporates the different literary styles and grammatical constructions of the Bible's human authors to communicate to different types of people.

- Jesus believed the Old Testament was inspired by God as evident that he attributed the Old Testament writings to the Holy Spirit, referred to Old Testament books as "Scripture(s)" from God, used "Scripture" and "God" interchangeably, and submitted himself to the authority of the Old Testament.

- The New Testament authors believed that the Old Testament was inspired by God as evident that they appealed to the Old Testament as Scripture, used "Scripture" and "God" interchangeably, attributed the Old Testament writings to the Holy Spirit, and their use of the Old Testament assumed inspiration.

Essay Questions

Short

1. Briefly explain each of the six theories of inspiration covered in this unit.

2. What complications does the modern usage of the word *inspiration* present?

3. What does Warfield say concerning Christianity as a revealed religion?

Long

1. Build the case for why verbal plenary inspiration is the only inspiration theory that is faithful to what Scripture says about itself.

Quiz

1. (T/F) The verbal plenary inspiration theory is the *only* theory that is faithful to what Scripture says of itself.

2. (T/F) The context of 2 Timothy 3:16 clearly conveys God breathing his words out to us.

3. (T/F) Per Warfield, the Bible's human authors were "creatively" active not "receptively active" in the writing of Scripture.

4. Which theory of inspiration posits that the Bible is unique when the Spirit utilizes it as a means of revelation within the community of God?

    a) The intuition theory
    b) The illumination theory
    c) The dynamic theory
    d) The encounter theory

5. With God's use of ordinary human means in mind, Abraham Kuyper and Herman Bavinck clarify that there is a(n) _____ nature to the inspiration of Scripture.

    a) Organic
    b) Mechanical
    c) Creative
    d) Active

6. Which term describes the all-extensive (*tota Scriptura*) nature of inspiration?

    a) Verbal
    b) Organic
    c) Receptive
    d) Plenary

7. Paul attributes inspiration to what?

    a) The human authors
    b) The Spirit using Scripture as a means of revelation
    c) The very words themselves
    d) The dictation of God's words

8. There is a _____ to Scripture, which means that each biblical book has both a divine author and a human author.

    a) Dual authority
    b) Dual authorship
    c) Dual inspiration
    d) Dual intuition

9. Which of the following statements does *not* argue that Jesus believed the Old Testament was inspired by God?

   a) Jesus used "God" and "Holy Spirit" interchangeably.
   b) Jesus attributed the Old Testament writings to the Holy Spirit.
   c) Jesus referred to Old Testament books as "Scripture(s)" from God.
   d) Jesus's enemies never questioned his belief that the Old Testament was inspired.

10. Which of the following is/are argument(s) that New Testament writers affirmed the Old Testament's divine inspiration?

   a) They used "Scripture" and "God" interchangeably.
   b) Their enemies never questioned their belief that the Old Testament was inspired.
   c) They were willing to be martyred on behalf of the gospel.
   d) They attributed the Old Testament writings to the Holy Spirit.
   e) Both A & D
   f) All of the above

CHAPTER 8

God Speaks Truthfully

The Inerrancy of Scripture

You Should Know

- Inerrancy means that Scripture, in its *autographa*, does not err in all that the biblical authors assert.

- Extractions from Feinberg's and Dockery's definitions of inerrancy: inerrancy requires humility; inerrancy means that Scripture is true in everything it affirms; inerrancy applies to the original autographs

- It is so important that the *autographa* be inerrant, because if the *autographa* is inerrant, then we can properly discern precisely where errors in transmission occurred.

- What is *not* necessary for inerrancy includes: strict adherence to the rules of grammar; exclusion of either figures of speech or of a given literary genre; verbal exactness when the New Testament cites the Old Testament; exhaustive comprehensiveness of any single account or of combined accounts

- Scripture can be completely truthful in what it asserts and affirms, without being totally precise.

- God's truthfulness identifies the true God from false gods, reflects his character, and is identified with God himself; God's trustworthiness and that of his speech are rooted in the doctrine of inspiration.

- Examples that prove Jesus's belief in the inerrancy of the Old Testament: he approached the Old Testament as true and factual; he treated the Old Testament as a unitary, comprehensive whole that does not contradict itself; he taught that the Old Testament could not be broken; he appealed to the Old Testament as that which is authoritative

- Limited inerrancy: The only place where Scripture is inerrant is in its central spiritual message.

- *Ipsissima vox Jesu*: the exact voice of Jesus

- The Chicago Statement on Inerrancy and the Cambridge Declaration explicitly link inerrancy with *sola Scriptura*.

Essay Questions
Short

1. Describe the three ways we see the "unbreakable chain" between God's trustworthiness and that of his Word.

2. In what ways did Jesus show his belief in the inerrancy of his own teachings? In what ways did the New Testament authors show their belief in the inerrancy of their writings?

3. What practical/ministerial issues arise if inerrancy is not upheld?

Long

1. What is inerrancy? Interact with Feinberg and Dockery in your answer. What does inerrancy have to do with *sola Scriptura*? Include discussions on "limited inerrancy" (particularly Sproul's hypothetical) and the fallibility of church councils, fathers, and popes (i.e., "what kind of authority do they possess?").

Quiz

1. (T/F) Inerrancy requires humility.

2. (T/F) Inerrancy demands that the *logia Jesu* contain only the *ipsissima vox* of Jesus, not the *ipsissima verba*.

3. (T/F) The New Testament authors believed that the Old Testament was inerrant but fallible.

4. (T/F) The connection between the trustworthiness of God and the trustworthiness of his speech is rooted in the doctrine of inspiration.

5. If the _____ is/are inerrant, then through the discipline of textual criticism we can properly discern precisely where errors in transmission occurred.

    a) Papyri
    b) Minuscules
    c) Autographa
    d) Majuscules

6. For Jesus, there is a _____ to Scripture that cannot be broken, and so Scripture must be treated as a unitary whole.

    a) Coherence
    b) Stream of consciousness
    c) Zeitgeist
    d) Grammatical precision

7. Jesus's _____, which was/were not derived from the Old Testament, reside(s) in his own person as the incarnate God-man.

    a) Miracles
    b) Authority
    c) Displays of power
    d) Ministry

8. This position argues that there are errors in Scripture, but when it comes to the Bible's central spiritual message, there are no errors.

    a) Limited atonement
    b) Limited infallibility
    c) Unlimited inerrancy
    d) Limited inerrancy

9. According to Luther, church councils, fathers, and popes possess a _____ authority at best.

    a) Derivative
    b) Ultimate

c) Equal
d) Inspired

10. Two church documents that explicitly link inerrancy with *sola Scriptura*?

a) Chicago Statement on Inerrancy
b) Cambridge Declaration
c) Westminster Confession of Faith
d) Belgic Confession

CHAPTER 9

God Speaks to Be Heard

The Clarity of Scripture

You Should Know

- God's written Word is not merely a revelation, but a communication.

- What is *not* true about scriptural clarity: every section of Scripture is easy to understand; everyone will understand the Bible; everyone will agree on how to interpret the Bible; each text is isolated on a hermeneutical island

- Four classes of audience were particularly targeted by the biblical authors: the uneducated, children, the church, and the Gentiles.

- Scripture attests to its own clarity in three ways: (1) It is meant for the *whole* assembly; (2) the New Testament's use of the Old Testament assumes Scripture's clarity; (3) the Bible's intended audience confirms its clarity.

- Locution: words spoken

- Illocution: the action performed by words

- Perlocution: the consequence or effect of the performed words

- The clarity of Scripture: Scripture is clear because God's speech is clear.

- Analogy of Scripture: Scripture is its own interpreter.

- Illumination: the term that denotes the Spirit's work of making the written Word's spiritual meaning clear to the individual reader

Essay Questions

Short

1. Why does a "plurality of interpretations" exist today? Do we find the same in the Bible? Explain your answer.

2. Explain how God's words do not just convey information, but they also perform an action.

3. How did Luther distinguish between external and internal clarity? How is this distinction a "helpful admonishment"?

Long

1. Discuss the clarity of God and his covenantal Word. Include a discussion of Scripture's efficacy and an overview of Scripture's witness to its own clarity.

Quiz

1. (T/F) The clarity of Scripture stems from the clarity of God.

2. (T/F) God's words do not merely convey information but perform actions as well.

3. (T/F) God's commands were not designed for the classroom but for everyday public conversation.

4. (T/F) The New Testament's use of the Old Testament assumes the clarity of Scripture.

5. One cannot miss the connection between God's Word and God's _____.

    a) Clarity
    b) Authority
    c) Law
    d) Presence

6. God's Word is irresistibly _____, successfully accomplishing the purpose for which it was sent.

a) Effective
b) Reliable
c) Dependable
d) Clear

7. We must also recognize that interpreters are _____.

a) Finite
b) Responsible
c) Humble
d) Objective

8. Internal clarity necessarily involves the work of the _____.

a) Son
b) Father
c) Holy Spirit
d) interpreter

9. _____ is the Spirit's work of taking the written Word and making its spiritual meaning clear to the individual reader.

a) Inspiration
b) Clarity
c) Inerrancy
d) Illumination

10. What was the Reformers' term for "Scripture interprets Scripture"?

a) "Scripture alone"
b) "Always reforming"
c) "Analogy of Scripture"
d) "Words of Jesus"

CHAPTER 10

God's Speech Is Enough
The Sufficiency of Scripture

You Should Know

- General revelation is sufficient to condemn, but insufficient to save.

- Sufficiency means that all things necessary for God's glory, salvation, and the Christian life are in Scripture. Sufficiency means that nothing should be added to the Bible. Sufficiency does not preclude the inward illumination of the Holy Spirit. Sufficiency does not annihilate general revelation.

- Biblical passages that show how Scripture's sufficiency is a doctrine that Scripture itself teaches: Deuteronomy 4:2, Revelation 22:18–19, Romans 15:4, 2 Timothy 3:14–17

- Two steps must be taken whenever we utilize extrabiblical sources: First, we must recognize from the start that they are fallible and imperfect; second, we must never use them independently of Scripture.

- We avoid evangelicalism's general allergy to tradition as exemplified by Alexander Campbell in two ways: (1) Guard against an individualistic mindset, and (2) recognize that tradition, insofar as it is consistent with Scripture, can and should act as a ministerial authority.

- Rome affirms Tradition 2, which states that both Scripture and unwritten oral tradition are sources of divine, infallible revelation.

- The council of Vatican II concludes that tradition, Scripture, and the church's teaching authority are "so joined together that one cannot stand without the others."

- Contra Rome, the church does not have an originating role with regard to Scripture. The church's role is best described as derivative and instrumental.

- Sufficiency of Scripture: All things necessary for God's glory, salvation, and the Christian life are given to us in the Scriptures.

- The light of nature: the natural revelation that serves to assist, inform, guide, and instruct us

Essay Questions

Short

1. How we do avoid the common evangelical mistake of discarding tradition?

2. How do Calvin's illustrations (i.e., "Scripture exhibits fully as clear evidence of its own truth as white and black things do of their color, or sweet and bitter things do of their taste") remind us of Scripture's self-authenticating nature?

3. Critique the "we-now-know-better" hermeneutic of Enns and Sparks.

Long

1. Referencing the Westminster Assembly's definitions from the Shorter Catechism and the Westminster Confession of Faith, explain what scriptural sufficiency means and what it does not mean.

Quiz

1. (T/F) The sufficiency of Scripture is synonymous with *sola Scriptura*.

2. (T/F) The Bible is unnecessary for the Church's *being*, that is, its very existence.

3. (T/F) One of the major problems conservatives had with liberals in the twentieth century was the latter taking their cue from culture rather than Scripture.

4. _____ means that all things necessary for God's glory, salvation, and the Christian life are provided for God's people in the Scriptures.

    a) Clarity
    b) Inerrancy
    c) Sufficiency
    d) Inspiration

5. The _____, in their response to Paul's message, assumed that Scripture is the final authority and that Scripture is enough.

    a) Bereans
    b) Thessalonians
    c) Romans
    d) Corinthians

6. What step(s) must be taken whenever we utilize extrabiblical sources?

    a) Use them to scrutinize our interpretation of Scripture.
    b) Place them on level ground with Scripture.
    c) Acknowledge that they are fallible and imperfect.
    d) Realize that we can never use them independently of Scripture.
    e) Both C & D
    f) All of the above

7. Cardinal Ratzinger (Pope Benedict XVI) once said, "Scripture is *not* _____ but at most only a *part* of the latter's greater reality."

    a) Revelation
    b) Tradition
    c) Inspiration
    d) Ultimate authority

8. God's Word is _____, that is, it does not depend upon a higher authority for its verification.

    a) Self-authorizing
    b) Self-authenticating

c) Self-interpreting

d) Self-revealing

9. The Enlightenment mentality that we can approach the Bible free from cultural presuppositions was rightly critiqued and shown wanting by _____.

a) Foundationalism

b) Rationalism

c) Empiricism

d) Postmodernism

10. Which is *not* one of sufficiency's implications for real life?

a) Sufficiency moves the believer from mere head knowledge to action.

b) Sufficiency is a fountain of comfort for the minister and the layperson.

c) Sufficiency reminds us that God's Word is to take center stage in the church.

d) Sufficiency reveals the truth of Scripture to the recipient.

ANSWER KEY

1. F, 2. F, 3. T, 4. C, 5. A, 6. E, 7. A, 8. B, 9. D, 10. D

Conclusion

Essay Questions

Short

1. What would happen to us if God did not speak with authority in his written Word?

2. How must we approach people and the Bible in light of the human heart's darkness?

3. What is covenant theology, and how has it illuminated God's Word for you?

Long

1. In the spirit of *semper reformanda* ("always reforming"), name some ways the church can continue to reform, according to the Word of God, and explain why. [Limit your discussion to topics covered in this course, such as *sola Scriptura* (inspiration, inerrancy, clarity, and sufficiency), postmodernism, Enlightenment thought, covenant theology, etc.]

Notes

www.ingramcontent.com/pod-product-compliance
Lightning Source LLC
Chambersburg PA
CBHW010921040426
42445CB00017B/1940